Contents

How to use the CD-ROM

The CD-ROM contains a PDF file labelled 'Worksheets.pdf' which consists of worksheets for each session in this resource. You will need Acrobat Reader version 3 or higher to view and print these pages.

The document is set up to print to A4 but you can enlarge the pages to A3 by increasing the output percentage at the point of printing using the page set-up settings for your printer.

Introduction and Rationale

This resource introduces a programme, called 'Girl's World', to support high school girls in developing their confidence, self-esteem and self-awareness. A major focus is also placed upon the development of emotional literacy and the ways in which girls can effectively contribute to peer support structures and mechanisms which aid the inclusion of all girls in both the social and school arenas. It was originally developed for, and delivered to, a group of girls within the context of a Pupil Referral Unit. However, given that the issues and content covered are obviously pertinent to all girls, we have compiled the ten sessions into a programme, which can be delivered to both smaller groups and whole classes of girls at high school level.

The Changing Roles of Women

In today's society, a view prevails that women can 'have it all' and it seems that young women and girls are generally hoping to strive for this status. They are continually bombarded by the media with images that communicate the diversity of women's lives, from successful banker to the high profile newsreader, and the successful singer married to a well-known footballer with the added appendages of a perfect family. It seems that women are, apparently, a success and that they will continue to be able to maintain such a position within society.

There is no doubt that women's lives have changed from being bound up with traditional expectations within the home context to having greater opportunities outside the home, and this seems to have brought a greater sense of self-belief and self-esteem for some women. The change can also be seen in the greater number of women in the workforce and the decline in the United Kingdom birth rate. Adams (1997) points out that 'over the past years, we have seen a supposed era of post-feminism'. However, Adams also acknowledges this period with caution in that it would seem that women's and young girls' lives have achieved their desired goals. Most importantly, the statistics would suggest that the achievement of equality is no longer a consideration when thinking about the direction of women and young girls' lives.

One area in which girls appear to have achieved enormous success is in the education system. The Office for Standards in Education (OFSTED) collaborated with the Equal Opportunities Commission in 1996 compiling a paper entitled 'The Gender Divide' which presented the following information:

- Girls out-perform boys at ages of 7, 11 and 14 years in National Curriculum assessments in English. Achievements in Mathematics and Science are broadly similar.

- Girls are more successful than boys at every level in GCSE – more achieve at least one Grade G or above. More achieve at least five Grade G or above. More achieve at least one Grade C or above. More achieve at least five Grade C or above and more achieve Grade A*.

> Girls are more successful than boys in terms of achieving GCSE Grades A* to C in all major subjects (p 6). Educationalists and researchers have continued to acknowledge the academic success of girls during recent years. Marks (2001) identified that, 'In a few short years girls have overtaken boys in many aspects of their education. Girls are now performing better than boys on many tests of educational attainment throughout their school careers from the age of 7 years upwards and more girls than boys now go on to universities' (p 1).

The Role of the Media

A major influence on girls' and young women's lives is to be found within the media and specifically within magazines designed for them. The magazines that teenage girls buy communicate the ideas of romance, beauty and life-style choices. Many of the magazines are held up to provide answers to questions that girls have and aid them in defining who they are or even who they wish to become. Furthermore, they also define what experience girls should expect to be having. McRobbie (2000) illustrated how girls' youth culture is intrinsically linked to such magazines. She stated that 'the messages which these images and stories together produce are limited and ambiguous...' These are:

> The girl has to fight to get and keep her man.

> She can never trust another woman.

> Romance and being a girl are fun.

It would seem, therefore, that such a perspective and pressure is directly in opposition to the push for academic success and future success in the workplace. Although women and young girls seem to have become detraditionalised on some levels and more assertive in preparing for their futures within the context of social culture and economic changes, there still appears to be a huge drive to foster the image of girls as unacademic beings who generally need to maintain a good appearance and be evidently attractive to the opposite sex. This contradiction continues to present girls with a level of stress and dissonance within their lives.

Issues of Self-esteem

Pipher (1994) states that 'most pre-adolescent girls are marvellous company because they are interested in everything: sport, nature, people, music and books' (p 18). However, it also appears that 'something dramatic happens to girls in early adolescence. Just as planes and ships disappear mysteriously into the Bermuda Triangle, so the selves of girls go down in droves' (p 19). This description of girls' movement towards adolescence and into adulthood illustrates some of the difficulties that they will encounter in terms of loss of self-esteem and identity. It seems that girls tend to lose their essential essence of who they actually are and seek to find new identities from within the peer group and the wider social context. The pressures are enormous and the vulnerability of girls tends to make them more open to such pressures. It is at this point that issues of relational aggression become more apparent.

Issues of Relational Aggression

Girls have always appeared to have cliques and hierarchies and always gossiped, bitched and ostracised but according to some psychologists, there is a new form of non-physical cruelty, which is spreading through schools. This kind of cruelty is deemed to be so extreme that it has actually been given a new name: relational aggression. Amelia Hill and Edward Helmore described this new phenomenon in their article in the Observer on 3 March 2002. They described how experts are comparing our knowledge of this kind of psychological warfare now with the attention given to domestic violence 20 years ago.

'Though it's not on the same scale (as domestic violence), we believe that with relational aggression, the trajectory of awareness, common knowledge and demand for change will follow the same track' (Holly Nishimura – Assistant Director of the Pennsylvania-based Ophelia project, *The Observer* Article, 3 March 2002).

This lack of awareness is, according to Rosalind Wiseman (founder of the Washington-based 'Empower Program'), allowing the warfare to wage unhindered in playgrounds and classrooms where teachers either dismiss girl-on-girl cruelty as being less important than the more obvious and disruptive male aggression, or actually fail to notice it altogether. For Wiseman, relational aggression can have devastating and long-term effects on its victims. She believes that girls' relationships with each other are really the key to their survival but they can also be the key to their destruction. Therefore, one main aim of this programme is to promote positive peer support in relationships, and to make girls aware of this phenomenon of relational aggression and the ways in which they need to be alert and aware of being pulled into such behaviours and situations.

Although research in this area is in its infancy, relational aggression seems to develop when children transfer from their small, more intimate primary context to large impersonal secondary schools where anonymity is the order of each day. According to Adrienne Katz (executive director of Young Voice):

> In the midst of such faceless confusion, many children abandon all interest in academia and concentrate entirely on working to be accepted by a social group. It is particularly traumatic for girls, because they traditionally need more emotionally intimate relationships than boys, which take time to develop. (*Observer* 3 March 2002)

Research by the Department for Education and Skills (referred to in Observer 3 March 2002) found that despite government legislation passed in 1999 compelling all state schools to have a bullying charter, over one-third of girls said that they have been too afraid to go to school at some point in their lives.

The effects of such insidious aggression are traumatic and the long-term effects can also be quite devastating for the individuals involved. Kidscape have investigated this form of bullying (Kidscape Survey, 1999) and found that adults who were bullied as children carry the problems with them into later life, reporting low levels of self-esteem, suicidal thoughts and difficulties in relating to other people. For Wiseman, these kinds of behaviours are directly related to the development of girls' self-esteem and coping abilities:

> I have realised that it is the relationship between girls that is directly responsible for creating the low self-esteem that leads women towards abusive relationships, unwanted pregnancies, drug and alcohol addiction and a whole sub-set of poor self-image manifestations from anorexia to bulimia.

This programme aims to highlight these issues with the groups of girls targeted and to emphasise the importance of developing intimate relationships that are based upon mutual trust and support rather than pressure, aggression and bullying.

Mental Health Issues in the Concept of Emotional Literacy

A further aim of this programme is to promote the girls' levels of emotional literacy in order to also foster and protect their mental health. The latter is key given that, 'Since the 1940s the number of children experiencing mental ill health has increased to 1 in 5' (The Big Picture Report, 1999). This Mental Health Foundation report also stated that:

Mental health problems in children and young people will continue to increase unless there is a coherent and holistic programme implemented to develop the emotional and mental health of our children… Emotionally literate children are less likely to experience mental health problems and, if they develop them, are less likely to suffer long term. Emotional literacy is derived from a combination of parents, schools and wider social networks.

Daniel Goleman (1995) defines emotional literacy as, 'The capacity for recognising our own feelings and those of others, for motivating ourselves and for managing emotions within ourselves and in our relationships'. 'Consequently, this programme attempts to promote students' emotional literacy and mental health within the educational context whilst also promoting the notion of emotional learning as an important life-long goal in every sphere of life.

Objectives

The main objectives of this ten session programme are to:

- ▸ Encourage students to become more aware of the importance of supporting each other and the benefits of forming strong, positive bonds with other females.

- ▸ Develop students' understanding of emotional literacy and the importance of being aware of their feelings and being able to manage them effectively.

- ▸ Ensure that students understand the importance of self-motivation and positive thinking.

- ▸ Raise students' self-esteem.

- ▸ Develop students' self-assurance and confidence and ability to make their own decisions in life.

- ▸ Encourage students to become more aware of the impact that the media has on society's perception of females and on their own perceptions of themselves.

- ▸ Create an awareness of the need to keep safe and the definitions of safety.

- ▸ Enable students to further develop and appreciate the perspective of others – to empathise.

- ▸ Further develop the facilitator's awareness and understanding of a range of strategies to effectively manage one's self and one's emotions.

- ▸ Encourage the facilitators and support staff to adopt a consistent approach in terms of developing students' emotional literacy, social skills and self-esteem.

- ▸ Further encourage facilitators to review the current policy and practice in terms of managing the emotional, social and behavioural needs of students in their care.

- ▸ Further develop healthy initiatives and programmes, which promote inclusive practice for those students who present as being most at risk.

The success of this programme will clearly depend upon how closely these objectives are followed and achieved.

The Structure of the Programme

The programme is divided into ten sessions. Each session includes a description of the aims and activities as well as the activity sheets for students to complete. The sessions are arranged in the following sequence.

> Session 1 – Introduction
>
> Session 2 – Emotional Literacy
>
> Session 3 – Self-esteem and Positive Thinking
>
> Session 4 – Peer Pressure
>
> Session 5 – Friendship and Relationships
>
> Session 6 – Sex
>
> Session 7 – Role Models
>
> Session 8 – Being a Parent
>
> Session 9 – Drugs and Alcohol
>
> Session 10 – Evaluation and Looking Forward

The Structure of the Sessions

Apart from the initial introductory session, the sessions generally follow a similar structure as follows.

Introduction

The main aims of the session are recorded by the facilitator on a flip-chart or whiteboard and these are discussed with the students at the outset. The students usually then participate in an icebreaker activity which generally consists of thought storming the topic to be covered.

Talk Time

The talk time element of the session encourages students to develop their own problem-solving strategies. The students are presented with a scenario sheet in which a girl is experiencing a difficulty or problem. The students are then asked to consider a series of questions, which particularly focus on how the girl may find a solution to the dilemma that she is currently facing and how to deal more effectively with it. The students are asked to consider the problems as a whole group and then to engage in role-play activities, taking on the roles of the characters in the problem scenarios and acting out the problem and solution.

These are generally paired activities in which students can have a go at taking on the role of the girl with the problem and the other character in the scenario. Students are finally required to feedback to the group as a whole as to how they managed the activity and what they felt about it.

Activity Sheets

In order to further clarify and reinforce specific skills and concepts, the students are presented with a series of activity sheets. These can require students to work either individually, in pairs or in smaller groups. The aim of these activities is generally to promote the development of personal skills and particularly foster students' ability to co-operate and work effectively as a member of a group.

Plenary

During the final part of each session, the thought storming approach will be again utilised in order to elicit the students' views as to the usefulness of the session. Not only is this an opportunity to summarise the skills and concepts covered, but it is also important to encourage the students to reflect upon the usefulness of the tasks, and begin to identify ways in which they might be able to further develop their own skills. A list of key questions is usually provided in order to prompt thinking and encourage participation in this part of the session.

Using the Programme

The sessions can be used in a variety of ways, either with a small group or with the whole class. Although the programme has been developed within the context of a Pupil Referral Unit and subsequently used with smaller groups of students, it would be feasible to utilise these resources within a larger group and to adapt them as appropriate for specific groups of students.

When first trialling this programme, it was possible to allocate both the form tutor and the educational psychologist to the target group in order to deliver each of these sessions, and to provide ongoing weekly tutorial support with individual students. However, it does not necessarily follow that similar arrangements should, or could, be made in other contexts. The allocation of such resources and attempts to work in such a multi-disciplinary way, should be appropriate to each context. It is important to ensure that those delivering this programme have some interest in both emotional literacy and social and behavioural skills themselves, and that they are able to function within an emotionally literate and supportive environment. It is also useful if facilitators have had some experience of managing groups and some understanding of group processes.

Introduction

It is helpful to have the aims of each session written up on the flip-chart prior to the start of the session. These can then be on display in an accessible place in the room as the girls come in for the session. At the start of the session the facilitator should talk through each of the recorded aims. These are provided at the start of each session plan and can be adapted in order to suit specific groups as appropriate. The aims explain to the students what they can expect to encounter and learn. This is also an opportunity for the facilitator to field any questions and clarify new concepts or definitions with the students.

Icebreaker

At the start of each session there will be an icebreaker activity, which usually consists of a thought storming session. This is intended to break down any barriers and create a positive climate for the remainder of this session – each student will be contributing to this process and there are no rights or wrongs involved. This will then usually be followed by the talk time problem-solving activity where students are asked to consider a problem, work together in order to create a solution and then role-play the two individuals involved in creating the original problem. It is important to make the students aware of this structure and the fact that this will generally be consistent throughout the sessions.

In the introductory session, the students initially agree to group rules and it is vital that an appropriate amount of time is allocated for this aspect of the course so as to ensure ownership of the rules. This will also allow each student to then adhere to the rules in subsequent sessions. Reinforcing group rules prior to clarifying the aims of each session is also helpful.

Talk Time

In order to introduce each of the scenarios it may be helpful for the facilitator to read through the problem cards to the students. This would take any pressure off girls who have difficulties in the area of literacy skills development. It may also be useful for the facilitator to provide an example role-play for the students prior to asking them to engage in this task. If the group is run by two facilitators then this task becomes much easier. However, it may be that one or two members of the group feel confident enough to participate in this with the facilitator.

Activity Sheets

The facilitator can then introduce the activity sheets that aim to both clarify and reinforce the specific topic introduced within the session. The sheets are designed to require minimal amounts of recording such as drawing, writing or discussing. They can be stored in individual folders, which the girls can make up at the start of the programme. These can be designed individually and we would strongly encourage the facilitators to allow some additional time for this, as good presentation of the work involved will invariably raise the profile of the group and its focus.

It will be important to take note of students whose recording skills are under-developed in order to provide any additional peer or adult support during these activities. However, it is anticipated that the facilitator will be skilled in differentiation and therefore able to ensure access for all students regardless of their level of ability. It will also be helpful to emphasise and promote peer support, given that one of the aims of the project is to promote the positive and supportive relationships that girls so desperately need at this stage in their development.

Plenary

This part of the session encourages the students to feedback their ideas and responses on the activity sheets and to also focus on the main elements covered in the session. It may be helpful for the facilitator to briefly summarise the main concepts covered and to record any responses from the students on the flip-chart or whiteboard. This will allow for highlighting experiences, ideas and feelings that may be common to the majority of students while also reinforcing any useful or not so useful strategies. It will also encourage students to highlight any difficulties or concerns that they may have had and to further self-reflect upon their own skills and the best way of moving forward.

Looking Forward

As with all such group-based programmes, it will be essential to ensure that an appropriate level of support is provided for individual students who require it, once the sessions have been completed. It may be helpful to continue to provide some weekly tutorial support for targeted individuals should they request it. It may also be helpful to encourage the girls to continue with problem-solving group work, taking on the facilitators' roles themselves and providing a support network for each other, which can also be further supported by adults within the school context. We would also hope that, in the longer term, school staff will become more aware of the need to promote the self-esteem and emotional literacy of girls in particular, and of the need to guard against relational aggression and the ways in which such behaviours can have a detrimental effect on the mental and emotional health of the girls in their care.

Maintaining and fostering the kind of empathic and solution focused problem-solving approach highlighted within these sessions will go some way to achieving such a goal.

References

A report from the Office of Her Majesty's Chief Inspector of Schools and the Equal Opportunities Commission (1996) The Gender Divide – Performance difference between boys and girls at school – HMSO Publication Centre UK.

Adams, Jo with support and contributions from Carol Painter (1997) *Girlpower – how far does it go? A Resource and Training Pack on Young Women and Self-esteem*, Sheffield Centre for HIV and Sexual Health.

Dann, J. (2001) *Emotional Intelligence in a Week*, Oxford: Hodder and Stoughton.

Francis, B. (2000) *Boys, Girls and Achievement – Addressing the Classroom Issues*, London and New York Routledge/Falmer-Taylor and Francis Group.

Goleman, D. (1995) *Emotional Intelligence – Why it matters more than IQ*, London: Bloomsbury.

Hill, A. & Helmore, E. Mean Girls. *The Observer*. 3 March 2002.

Kidscape Survey: Long Term Effects of Bullying, November 1999.

Marks, J. (2001) *Girls Know Better – Educational Attainments of Boys and Girls*, Civitas: Institute for the Study of Civil Society: Harlington Fine Art Ltd., Sussex.

Marris, B. & Rae, T. (2004) *Escape from Exclusion*, Bristol: Lucky Duck Publishing.

McRobbie, A. (2000) *Feminism and Youth Culture*, 2nd Edition. Macmillan Press Ltd. Hampshire/London Printed in Hong Kong.

Pipher, Mary (1994) *Reviving Ophelia: Saving the selves of adolescent girls*, New York: Ballantine Books.

Plummer, G. (2000) *Failing Working-class Girls*. Staffordshire: Trentham Books Limited.

Rae, T. (2004) *Emotional Survival: An Emotional Literacy Programme for High School Students*, Bristol: Lucky Duck Publishing.

The Big Picture Report (1999) by the Mental Health Foundation, February.

Session 1

Introduction

The facilitator can outline the main aims of this session as follows:

- For students to become aware of the objectives and themes that will be examined in the sessions.

- For students to work together to agree on a set of rules for the course.

- For students and facilitator(s) to share their likes and dislikes with each other to learn more about themselves and to start building trusting relationships with each other.

In this initial session it will also be important for the facilitator to clarify the aims of the project as a whole. As this is the first session in the programme, it does not follow the usual structure of subsequent sessions.

The facilitator may wish to make use of the whiteboard or flip-chart in order to highlight the main objectives of the course as follows. Within the framework of the Girl's World programme the students will be encouraged to:

- Build up new friendships and consolidate their existing ones.

- Create a sense of trust and confidence in each other.

- Create a sense of belonging to a group.

- Develop their self-esteem and self-confidence.

- Extend their social skills in speaking and listening.

- Develop a positive attitude and maintain motivation.

- Develop empathy for others and promote understanding.

- Develop positive behaviours and the ability to self-reflect and modify behaviours.

- Become more assertive.

- Increase their level of emotional literacy and self-awareness.

The students will be asked to contribute to the series of ten sessions in order to develop their own skills and competencies, and to also learn how to work effectively as a part of a solution focused problem-solving group. The topics to be covered will include the following:

- Developing emotional literacy.

- Building self-esteem and positive thinking.

- Coping with peer pressure.

- Developing positive friendships and relationships.

- Developing a positive and safe attitude towards sex.
- Understanding role models.
- Issues around parenting.
- Issues around drugs and alcohol abuse.
- Maintaining motivation and setting realistic targets.

The facilitator may wish to also highlight the structure of subsequent sessions in which the girls will be asked to consider a range of problems that they themselves may have experienced, and to work together solving these problems via solution focused approaches and role-play activities. Sessions will usually follow a similar pattern as follows:

- A short introduction.
- An icebreaker.
- A talk time problem-solving activity.
- Work sheet activities.
- Plenary session.

This initial session does not follow the above sequence. The idea here is for a 'facilitator to get to know you' session in which girls can both reflect upon themselves and share their likes, dislikes and preferences with each other. It is also vital that group rules are set within this session so as to ensure the inclusion and safety of all students within subsequent sessions.

Icebreaker

In this session the icebreaker can take the form of a Circle Time activity in which the students can introduce themselves in turn, and identify three main points about themselves that they would like the others to know. This can then be further extended through a paired activity in which students are asked to question each other for two minutes each, in order to find out as many facts as possible about each other. These facts can then be fed back to the group via each of the partners in turn.

Activity 1 – My Personal Profile: All About Me

This activity builds upon the initial icebreaker activity in that it requires each student to complete a personal profile. The facilitator will need to have access to a digital camera so each student can have their photograph taken, and this can be presented on the front sheet of each of the Personal Profiles.

For the Positive Thoughts section of the Personal Profile the students are asked to identify three things that: excite them, they feel confident about, they want to know more about, always make them feel good, they really agree with, are their main interests and make them feel happy.

For the Negative Thoughts section of the Personal Profile they are asked to identify three things that: make them feel depressed, they feel worried about, they are just not interested in, make them feel down, make them feel angry, make them feel bored and make them feel unhappy.

For the final sheet of the Personal Profile students are firstly asked to look back at their answers to the Negative Thoughts section and to try to pick one negative from each group, and work out what they could do in order to cope better and reduce their negative feelings in this area.

Secondly, they are asked to stop, think and reflect upon who else could help them in these situations. Students will need time to discuss their ideas with a partner and then feedback the ways in which they are going to move forward to the group as a whole. The facilitator will need to be sensitive to each individual's current needs and levels of confidence. As with all activities that follow, students should have the opportunity to pass if they so desire.

Activity 2 – Setting Girl's World Group Rules

The group rules for these sessions need to be agreed and owned by all the students involved and should be reinforced at the beginning of each subsequent session. The facilitator can explain that rules should be identified in order to ensure the safety of every member of the group and to protect their self-esteem throughout the duration of the course. Students can be asked to contribute via a thought storming process in order to ensure that group rules are owned by all involved. These rules may include the following:

- ▸ Everyone needs to listen to each other.

- ▸ Everyone needs to take turns.

- ▸ Everyone needs to respect each other's space and ideas.

- ▸ Everyone has the right to pass.

- ▸ Everyone in the group needs to try to give ideas and offer solutions.

- ▸ Everyone needs to use their imagination.

- ▸ Everyone must be careful not to criticise others' ideas but to build upon them.

- ▸ Everyone must agree that what is talked about in the sessions will stay in the sessions, and will not be discussed with people outside the group.

For future sessions, the group rules can be recorded on the format provided. The facilitator may wish to enlarge this to A3 size in order to recall students' ideas during the session. However, it may be helpful for each student to have an A4 copy of the format so as to record the rules for themselves and file these in the individual folders or course books as appropriate.

Plenary

The facilitator may wish to focus on the following questions:

- ▸ What have we learnt about ourselves in this session?

- ▸ What have we learnt about each other in this session?

- ▸ How did we feel at the start of the session?

- ▸ How do we feel now at the end of the session?

My Personal Profile:

All About Me

Paste photo here

Name: _____ Age: _____

My Personal Profile
Positive Thoughts

Record your ideas, thoughts and feelings.

3 things that excite me:

- _____
- _____
- _____

3 things I feel confident about:

- _____
- _____
- _____

3 things I want to know more about:

- _____
- _____
- _____

3 things that always make me feel good:

- _____
- _____
- _____

3 things I really agree with:

- _____
- _____
- _____

3 of my main interests:

- _____
- _____
- _____

3 things that make me feel happy:

- _____
- _____
- _____

My Personal Profile
Negative Thoughts

Record your ideas, thoughts and feelings.

3 things that make me depressed:

- _____
- _____
- _____

3 things I feel worried about:

- _____
- _____
- _____

3 things I am just not interested in:

- _____
- _____
- _____

3 things that make me feel down:

- _____
- _____
- _____

3 things that make me feel angry:

- _____
- _____
- _____

3 things that make me feel bored:

- _____
- _____
- _____

3 things that make me feel unhappy:

- _____
- _____
- _____

My Personal Profile
Becoming More Positive

Look back at your answers on your **negative thoughts**. Try to pick one negative from each group and then work out what you could do in order to cope better and reduce your negative feelings.

Negative	Things I could do to become more positive and change the situation and feelings
1. I get depressed about:	
2. I worry about:	
3. I am not interested in:	
4. I feel down about:	
5. I feel angry about:	
6. I get bored when:	
7. I feel unhappy about:	

Stop, think and reflect

Who else can help you? What could they do? Discuss your ideas with a partner and then feedback to the whole group.

Girl's World Group Rules

We all agree to keep the following rules in our Girl's Group:

○ _____

○ _____

○ _____

○ _____

○ _____

○ _____

Signed: (_____)   Date: (_____)

Introduction

The facilitator can outline the main aims of this session as follows:

- ▸ For students to become aware of the skills required to becoming emotionally literate.

- ▸ For students to understand the importance of empathy and other skills of emotional literacy.

- ▸ For students to reflect on their skills of emotional literacy and think of ways of improving.

In this session the facilitator will be introducing the concept of emotional literacy. This concept will initially be introduced via a story and follow on activity in which students are asked to identify which characters they deemed to have the nastiest qualities. At this stage, many of the students may not have heard of, or particularly understand, the concept of emotional literacy and this is why the introductory part of the session involves the story being read aloud by the facilitator to the whole group.

The story focuses on two girls who go on holiday together and decide to take a walk on a rather stormy day. As the storm gets worse they decide that they need to take shelter. One girl runs across a bridge, which then collapses. This leaves the other girl exposed to the elements and extremely scared, having no means of real shelter and no food or water available to her as they had been taken across the bridge by her friend. The friend finds that she can shelter inside some caves and subsequently decides to have a little picnic, seemingly unconcerned of her friend's needs across the ravine. In the meantime a waiter from the hotel appears, having followed the girls in order to warn them of the ensuing storm. He finds one of them stranded underneath a tree and asks her what has happened to her friend. This girl is very much attracted to the waiter, and she says that her friend is stuck over the other side. The waiter then suggests that the two of them get together since he had always been attracted to her as well.

Read the story

This story is meant to be tongue-in-cheek and very light-hearted and the facilitator should read this with this fact in mind.

Activity 1 - Talk Time

The facilitator then divides the girls into small groups and asks them to work together in order to identify the nastiest person in this story, the second nastiest person in the story, and the third nastiest person in the story. The activity sheet entitled The Greek Adventure is provided as a prompt. They are asked to do this by arranging themselves in circles with one student beginning by offering their ideas and ranking order. The student sitting next to her on the right-hand side has to summarise the first girl's views before then offering her own. Once everyone has had a go at summarising each other's views and offering their own views, the facilitator asks each group to see if they can reach an agreement on the rankings that they have. They can then feedback their ideas to the group as a whole.

Activity 2 – Thought Storming Activity

The facilitator then asks the group to identify the skills that they were using during this problem-solving activity. The idea here is to begin to identify the skills of emotional literacy and learn that these are skills that we have to make use of daily, in order to both engage with each other and ensure the development and maintenance of appropriate relationships. Students may offer some of the following contributions:

- listening skills
- turn taking
- withholding gratification
- managing our feelings
- showing empathy to others
- eye contact
- problem-solving
- accepting difference
- assertiveness
- conflict resolution.

Activity 3 – Definitions

The facilitator can then highlight the fact that these skills are all part of this notion of emotional literacy. This concept can then be further clarified by the Definitions sheet. Emotional literacy is defined as follows: Recognising, understanding, appropriately expressing and effectively managing emotions in ourselves and in relationships with others (Marris and Rae 2004). People who are emotionally literate are able to get on with others, resolve conflicts, motivate themselves and achieve in life.

The facilitator can further highlight the key skills of emotional literacy as follows: Awareness of your feelings, self-assurance, authenticity, flexibility, personal insight, self-regulation, accountability and self-motivation (Dann 2001).

The students can then be asked to work in pairs in order to try and formulate their own definitions for each key skill. They need to have access to dictionaries or thesauruses and ideas can be recorded by students on separate sheets.

Activity 4 – How Are Your Skills?

This activity requires students to complete a self-evaluation quiz in which they rate their own level of competency in each of the key areas of emotional literacy. Most important is that students are given the opportunity to understand that the key skills are the skills that they will need to develop in order to survive within all social contexts. It is important to emphasise the need to become a self-reflective person who can continually identify key areas for change and development. Being able to continually develop emotional, social and behavioural skills is really the key to ensuring success for students both socially and academically.

Plenary

The facilitator may wish to focus on the following questions:

- ▸ What were your strengths and weaknesses according to the quiz?

- ▸ Were you surprised by any of the results?

- ▸ What have you decided to do to improve your skills?

The Greek Adventure

Once upon a time, there were two girls called Kylie and Sharon. They went on a holiday to a great Greek island where there were loads of cool things to do and loads of hot guys to meet. They had two weeks just to have a laugh and a really good time together.

At the start of their second week, they decided that they had both put on too much weight from all the drinking, eating and lazing around the pool. So, they decided to go for a walk across the coastal path in order to burn off a few calories and get ready for the next night's drinking and clubbing.

As they walked around the northern ridge, they could feel the sun beating down on their heads. It was really hot so they decided to stop for a drink of water.

'I can feel myself dehydrating,' said Kylie. 'It must be the effects of last night's drinking.' She gulped down some water and passed the bottle to Sharon.

'Thanks,' said Sharon sarcastically, 'you haven't exactly left me enough to quench my thirst!'

'Don't start,' said Kylie. She was just about to launch into an argument, telling Sharon how selfish she was and how she always had to go first and have her own needs met first. However, she suddenly saw something out at sea. She stood still and stared straight ahead, her mouth slightly gaping.

'What is it?' said Sharon, sounding confused and somewhat perturbed that Kylie had stopped mid-flow as she was secretly looking forward to the ensuing argument. She turned around and followed Kylie's gaze to the sea.

'Oh my God!' she said. The storm was clearly visible on the horizon, the dark clouds had formed within what seemed like seconds and the thunder had erupted into great blasts overhead.

'I think we'd better run for it,' said Kylie. 'We seem to be far too exposed on this ridge.' Sharon nodded in agreement.

'Look down there in the valley – there's a bridge across to some caves. We'd probably be better off if we got down there. At least we would have some shelter.' 'Come on then,' said Kylie, 'let's make a run for it.'

They proceeded to scramble down the rough goat track until they reached the bridge, which was a rather rickety affair. Sharon thought that it wasn't likely to hold their weight but also thought she'd better keep her thoughts to herself. She'd only be accused of being negative yet again.

Kylie ran ahead of her and shouted back, 'Come on! Hurry up! The storm seems to be getting stronger! Head for the cave!'

She ran onto the bridge and straight across it. Just as she reached the other end, the bridge collapsed entirely leaving Sharon stranded on the other side of the ravine.

Kylie turned around and watched in utter horror as it shattered into pieces. The wood was absolutely rotten. Sharon stood still, biting her lip. For one moment she considered trying to jump across and then immediately thought the better of it. You'd need to be an Olympic medallist to cope with that.

Kylie shouted to her, 'Get back behind the trees. Find the biggest one and sit under it with your back against the trunk! Go on! Hurry up!'

She ran off into the cave. Fortunately, she had been carrying the rucksack containing all the food for their lunch and she now thought that she would sit down, dry off and have a little picnic. She remembered that she had packed two small bottles of Chardonnay and felt quite pleased with herself.

Sharon ran back to find shelter under the clump of trees and sat down. She did not feel happy or particularly safe from the storm. She's the one that is entirely selfish, she thought, and I've broken three nails scrambling down that hill.

Just then she heard a rustle in the undergrowth behind her. She sat up feeling startled and frightened, thinking there would be a snake nearby and then let out a big sigh of relief as she saw the head waiter from the hotel approaching her. He was absolutely gorgeous – tall, handsome, with quite exceptional pectoral muscles.

'Hello Ramiro,' she said, 'what on earth are you doing out in a storm like this?' 'Well,' he replied, 'I saw you both leave for your walk and I ran after you because I heard the appalling weather forecast. I was hoping to catch up with you both and warn you. Are you okay?' 'Yes I am now,' she said.

'But where is your friend?' asked Ramiro. 'Oh,' she replied, looking somewhat dejected, 'she's stuck over the other side. She was too fat and unfit to get over here.' 'Oh dear,' said Ramiro, 'Well, suppose it's not such a bad thing really.' 'What do you mean?' said Sharon rather shocked.

'Well, I've always fancied you. Now that she is out of the picture we should be able to get to know each other properly. What do you think?' 'Okay,' she said and jumped directly into his arms, kissing his neck and his chest repeatedly.

I'm afraid the rest of it simply can't be recorded here.

THE END

Talk Time

The Greek Adventure

On your own, identify:

- The **nastiest** person in the story.

- The 2nd **nastiest** person in the story.

- The 3rd **nastiest** person in the story.

Now work in your group to reach an agreement on the rankings.

Going around the circle, give your views one at a time.

(The girl on the right of the first speaker should listen and summarise the first girl's views before she gives her own. Then the girl sitting on her right has to do the same and so on.)

Feed back to the group as a whole.

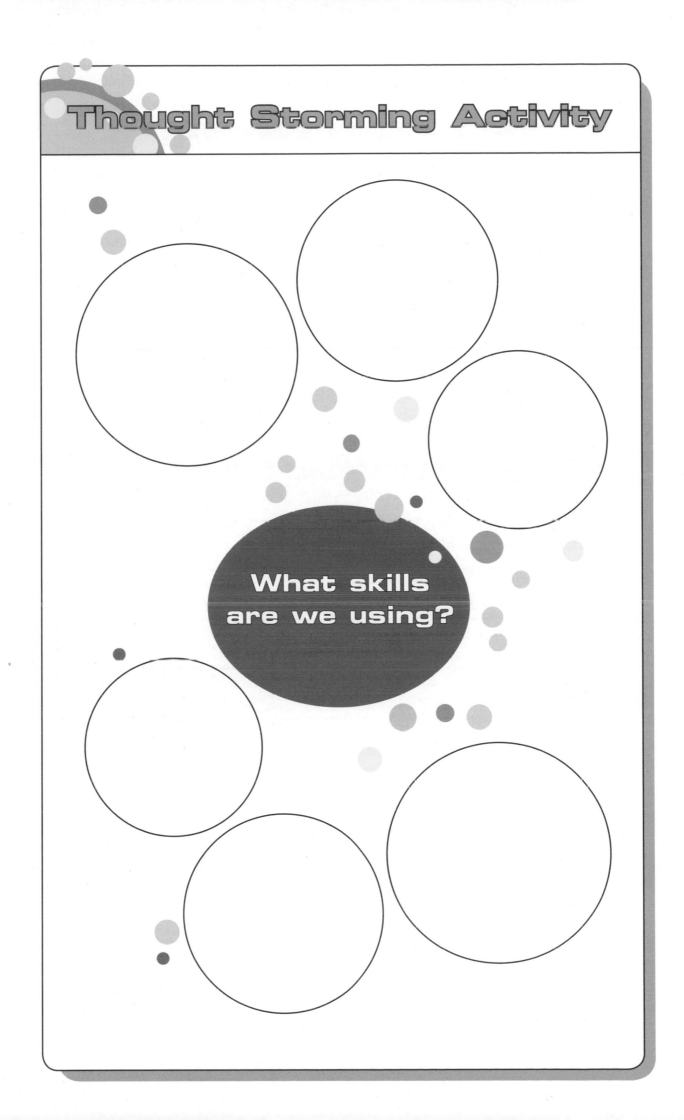

Emotional Literacy

- Recognising, understanding, appropriately expressing and effectively managing emotions in ourselves and in relationships with others.

- People who are emotionally literate are able to get on with others, resolve conflicts, motivate themselves and achieve in life.

Key Skills of Emotional Literacy

Awareness of your feelings	
Personal insight	
Self-assurance	
Authenticity	
Flexibility	
Self-regulation	
Accountability	
Self-motivation	

In the space provided, try to come up with your own definitions of these words with a partner. Use a dictionary and record your ideas.

How Is Your Emotional Literacy?

How do you rate? Read each statement and tick against each scale:

0 = not at all   3 = sometimes   5 = always

Under each heading add your score to get a total score out of 20.

Awareness of feelings

	0	1	2	3	4	5
You know what you are feeling						
You can label your feelings						
You know when your feelings affect your work						
You know when your feelings affect your relationships						

TOTAL SCORE: /20

Personal insight

	0	1	2	3	4	5
You know your strengths						
You know your weaknesses						
You can take constructive criticism or feedback from others						
You know when you've done something well and can feel good about yourself						

TOTAL SCORE: /20

Self-assurance

	0	1	2	3	4	5
You act confidently in most situations						
You stick up for things you think are right						
Other people think you are confident						
You could easily name three things you are good at even when you are down						

TOTAL SCORE: /20

How Is Your Emotional Literacy?
continued

Self-regulation or control

	0	1	2	3	4	5
You can stop yourself when you know you're behaving in a way that will cause problems (for you and others)						
You can keep calm under pressure						
You can handle uncomfortable feelings well						
You can use strategies to reduce stress and anxiety						

TOTAL SCORE: /20

Authenticity

	0	1	2	3	4	5
When you say you'll do something you do it						
You don't say or act one thing and then do another						
You can admit your mistakes						
You can stand up for what you think even if you are in the minority						

TOTAL SCORE: /20

Accountability

	0	1	2	3	4	5
You can take responsibility for your behaviour and actions						
You keep your promises						
You admit when you have made a mistake						
Your friends and family know they can count on you						

TOTAL SCORE: /20

How Is Your Emotional Literacy?
continued

Flexibility

	0	1	2	3	4	5
You can cope with changes to your day						
You don't get stressed by change and can go with the flow						
You like to be creative and think of new ways of doing things						
You see the benefit in trying new things and are eager to do so						

TOTAL SCORE: /20

Self-motivation

	0	1	2	3	4	5
You like to achieve your best						
You like to get things done						
You are committed to your relationships						
You'll keep going even if things get tough						
You are optimistic and look for opportunities before you look for problems						

TOTAL SCORE: /20

Stop and Think

What are your highest scores?

Where are your lowest scores?

Which is your best key skill and which is your weakest?

Try to think of three things that you could do in order to improve your skills:

1) _____

2) _____

3) _____

Introduction

The facilitator can outline the main aims of this session as follows:

- ▸ For students to be able to identify their own levels of self-esteem and to understand the concept of self-esteem.

- ▸ For students to understand how what others say can affect our self-esteem and levels of confidence.

- ▸ For students to understand the importance of motivation and positive thinking.

The facilitator will be aware that there are many definitions of self-esteem and none is definitive. However, it may be helpful to make reference to the California Task Force to Promote Self-esteem's 1990 definition as follows:

'Appreciating my own worth and importance and being accountable for myself and my responsibilities towards others.'

The facilitator may also wish to highlight alternative definitions of self-esteem as follows:

- ▸ a positive belief in my own value as an individual, which is both enabling and empowering

- ▸ knowing myself and my capabilities

- ▸ knowing I have rights and deserve love and respect

- ▸ feeling confident enough to cope with life's pressures and changes

- ▸ feeling secure in myself

- ▸ feeling worthy of my own happiness.

Activity 1 – Thought Storming Activity

In this activity students are required to thought storm the following:

What is self-esteem?

Ideas can be recorded on the sheet provided, either individually or allocating one member of the group to act as scribe. The facilitator may wish to scribe the students' views on a whiteboard or flip-chart as opposed to making use of the framework provided. Most important is to ensure that the students have the opportunity to make their own definitions, which will consequently be more amenable to them than one that is imposed.

Talk Time

Students are presented with a scenario sheet in which a student is experiencing a difficulty as regards her level of self-esteem. The scenario involves one girl's difficulties with her weight and the way in which others perceive her. The students are asked to consider a series of questions, which particularly focus on how this girl may improve her self-esteem and self-image and cope more effectively with the negative comments of others.

Activity 2 – What Do They Say?

In this activity students are asked to consider how others affect their self-esteem in both negative and positive ways. They are asked to identify something that each individual has said about them and how this made them feel, focusing on parents/carers, friends, teachers, brothers, sisters or cousins themselves and one other individual.

Activity 3 – Bingo Build-up

This activity is designed to facilitate and promote a more positive ethos in the group after Activity 2, which could engender some negative feelings and dampen the group ethos to some extent. The Bingo Build-up activity asks students to move around the group finding at least one person who meets the criteria in each of the boxes on the sheet. The person then has to sign the box, and students are asked to continue this activity until everyone in the group has filled in as many boxes as possible. This is a very simple and fun activity, which is safe as it asks students to reflect on entirely positive points in themselves and others.

Activity 4 – Turn the Negatives to Positives

In this activity students are asked to consider how we can frequently make ourselves feel negative or we can talk ourselves down. It is important that we begin to stop, think and reflect and to analyse the extent to which we engage in this kind of negative self-talk. Students are asked to look at a series of negative statements and then to work with a partner in order to try and turn them into positives.

Plenary

The facilitator can encourage the students to focus upon the following questions:

▸ How did we feel at the start of this session?

▸ How do we feel now?

▸ What do we think we have learnt about our self-esteem?

▸ What do we think we have learnt about the importance of positive thinking?

▸ How do we think our experiences today will help us in the future?

Thought Storming Activity

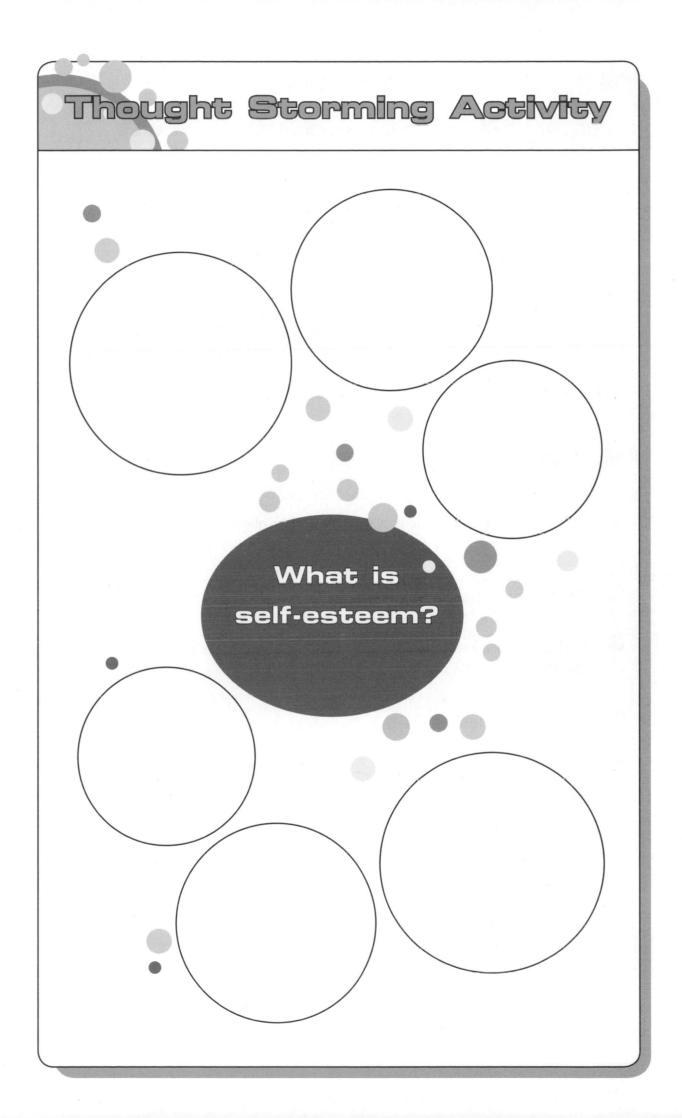

What is self-esteem?

Scenario: Self-esteem

Natalie has always been worried about her weight and it doesn't help that her best friend is really slim and is always noticed by the boys.

So recently, Natalie has become more interested in her appearance and she has begun to buy teen and fashion magazines. She spends a lot of time looking at the possible outfits that she could buy and admiring the slim bodies of the models and celebrities.

One day while Natalie was hanging about with her best friend Trisha, Natalie showed her some of the clothes she was thinking about buying in the magazines. Trisha giggled and kidded, 'You can't wear that your stomach will be hanging over!'

Questions

○ What are the different ways in which Natalie could react to that comment?

○ Do you think that Trisha cares about Natalie's weight?

○ Is there a different way in which Trisha could have worded her statement?

○ Does Natalie feel ugly?

○ In which ways could Natalie improve the way she feels about herself (self-esteem)?

○ Does Trisha's comment say more about how Trisha feels about herself?

○ What should Natalie do now that she knows what her friend thinks about her?

○ Is Trisha a good friend?

What Do They Say?

People can affect our self-esteem in both negative and positive ways. What they say can have a real impact upon our feelings. Try to identify something that each of the following people have said about you and how they made you feel.

Parent/carer	Friend	Teacher
They said…	They said…	They said…
I felt…	I felt…	I felt…

Brother/sister/cousin	Myself	Other
They said…	They said…	They said…
I felt…	I felt…	I felt…

Bingo Build-up

Complete the Bingo Build-up Chart by talking to everyone in the group. Try to find at least one person who meets the criteria from each box. The person then has to sign the box. Carry on until everyone in the group has filled in as many boxes as possible.

Is good at running	**Was born in March**	**Likes animals**
Can speak another language	**Likes the sun**	**Has at least one sister**
Has met a famous person	**Is a Capricorn**	**Likes the same food as you**
Likes going on the Internet	**Is good at English**	**Can play a musical instrument**
Keeps fit	**Has a tattoo**	**Has blue eyes**
Like listening to music	**Has a computer**	**Has black hair**

Turn the Negatives to Positives

We make ourselves feel negative when we talk ourselves **down**.

Look at the negative statements. Work with a partner and try to turn them into positives.

Negative Comment	Positive Comment
I'm fat and ugly	
No-one ever asks me out	
Other girls have better clothes than me	
Everyone is better looking than me	
I'm just no good at school work	
My teachers think I'm a stupid lump	

Introduction

The facilitator can outline the main aims of this session as follows:

▸ For students to understand peer pressure and examine situations in which it is used.

▸ For students to be able to distinguish between passive, aggressive and assertive behaviour and understand the importance of being assertive in peer pressure situations.

▸ For students to reflect on how they would cope and deploy assertive behaviours in a variety of situations.

It will initially be helpful to consider the concept of peer pressure and perhaps to offer students a couple of definitions as follows:

▸ Peer pressure is when you feel vulnerable to giving in to the opinions of others.

▸ Peer pressure is when you feel pressure to go along with the crowd when you don't really want to.

This should help to prompt students' thinking for the subsequent thought storming activity.

Activity 1 – Icebreaker: Thought Storming Activity

Students are asked to focus on the following question:

What is peer pressure and when do we experience this?

Students can either record their views on the activity sheet provided or the facilitator may wish to record students' views on the whiteboard or flip-chart. What is most important is for students to formulate their own definitions in order to ensure that these are owned and entirely meaningful to them.

Talk Time: Problem-solving Activity

Students are presented with the scenario in which a student has moved to a new area. She is asked by a group of girls at her new school to go shopping during the weekend in order to get some new make-up. Whilst they are in the shop, one of her new friends steals some mascara. During the next shopping trip the same friend tries to pressurise Günsel into stealing a lipstick. The students are asked to consider a range of questions and different outcomes to this problem prior to engaging in the role-play activity.

Role-play

Students are divided into pairs and asked to role-play the problem, working out the conversation between Suzie and Günsel and focusing on how Günsel can resist this peer pressure. Students can take it in turns to take on the role of each of the students and then feedback to the rest of the group how difficult or otherwise they found this particular problem to solve. Once again it is important to encourage students to develop appropriate scripts to resist this kind of peer pressure.

Activity 2 – Being Assertive

This activity aims to encourage the students to behave more assertively and to particularly understand the distinction between assertive, aggressive and passive responses. It may be helpful for the facilitator to model or act out these behaviours – perhaps by making use of the following approaches:

▸ asking to leave the room in an assertive, aggressive and passive way

▸ asking an imaginary person to give her/him their phone back

▸ telling the teacher that she was not responsible for breaking the ruler.

The facilitator can ask students to pay attention to body language, tone and volume of voice, facial expression and so on. This should help prompt students' responses on the Being Assertive activity sheet, where they are asked to consider how they would look, think and act if they were being (a) assertive, (b) aggressive and (c) passive.

Activity 3 – Peer Pressure Cards

Students are presented with a series of Peer Pressure Cards, which can have been cut out and laminated prior to the start of the session by the facilitator. The twelve pressures are as follows:

1. The pressure to bunk school.

2. The pressure to take drugs.

3. The pressure to get smashed.

4. The pressure to shop-lift.

5. The pressure to go joy-riding.

6. The pressure to bully someone.

7. The pressure to have sex with someone.

8. The pressure to give someone your money.

9. The pressure to diet.

10. The pressure to mess about in lessons.

11. The pressure to be rude to other people or neighbours.

12. The pressure to lie to your parents or carers.

Students are asked to participate in this activity via the Circle Time approach. Each girl can pick one card at a time, reading it aloud and then trying to answer the following key questions posed by the facilitator. These key questions are recorded on the key question sheet. This can be enlarged to A3 size or, alternatively, the key questions can be written up on the whiteboard or flip-chart. These are as follows:

▸ What do you think you would do if you were under pressure to do this? How would you feel?

▸ What would make you give in to the pressure?

▸ What would help you to resist the pressure?

▸ How do you think you would feel afterwards if you gave in to the pressure?

- What do you think would happen if you refused to give in or get involved? How would you feel?

- How would you cope with the situation?

- What would be the benefits to you of not getting involved?

- What would be the benefits to others of you not getting involved?

Plenary

The facilitator can ask the students to focus on the following questions:

- How did you feel at the start of this session?

- How do you feel now?

- What do you think you have learnt about peer pressure in this session?

- Do you think you have developed any skills that will help you to cope with peer pressures more effectively in the future – if so can you identify these?

Thought Storming Activity

What is peer pressure and when do we experience this?

Talk Time

Scenario: Peer Pressures

Günsel has recently moved to a new area. The group of girls at her new school has asked her to go to the shopping centre to get some new make-up.

In the shop they are comparing and trying on the make-up when Suzie stuffs some mascara into her jacket pocket. Suzie whispers, 'Don't say anything,' and they quickly leave the store.

On the next trip to the same shop, they are looking at lipsticks when Suzie says, 'It's your turn, put this in your bag.'

Questions

○ What should Günsel do?

○ Is Suzie a good friend?

○ What would happen if they were caught?

○ Would you know how to get out of this situation?

○ Would you ever use peer pressure to make someone do something you wanted them to do?

○ What is Günsel feeling?

○ What is Suzie feeling?

○ What will Suzie tell other people?

○ Name some other instances when teenagers use peer pressure.

Being Assertive

We can cope best with peer pressure if we are assertive and not passive or aggressive. Thought storm! How would you **feel**, **look** and **act** if you were being:

(a) Assertive

(b) Aggressive

(c) Passive

Complete the chart and share your ideas.

	Assertive	Aggressive	Passive
How would you feel?			
How would you look?			
How would you act?			

Practise Being Assertive

Use the Peer Pressure Cards in order to practise your skills and make positive choices!

Pressure 1 To bunk school	**Pressure 2** To take drugs
Pressure 3 To get smashed	**Pressure 4** To shop-lift
Pressure 5 To bully someone	**Pressure 6** To go joy-riding
Pressure 7 To have sex with someone	**Pressure 8** To give someone your money
Pressure 9 To mess about in lessons	**Pressure 10** To diet
Pressure 11 To be rude to others/neighbours	**Pressure 12** To lie to your parents/carers

Peer Pressure Cards

Key Questions

Girls can pick one card at a time, read it out and then try to answer the following key questions:

1. What do you think you would do if you were under pressure to do this? How would you feel?

2. What would make you give in to the pressure?

3. What would help you resist the pressure?

4. How do you think you would feel afterwards if you gave in to the pressure?

5. What do you think would happen if you refused to give in and get involved? How would you feel?

6. How would you cope with the situation?

7. What would be the benefits to you if you didn't get involved?

8. What would be the benefits to others of you not getting involved?

Introduction

The facilitator can outline the main aims of this session as follows:

> ▸ For students to understand the importance of friendship and the nature of positive relationships.

> ▸ For students to examine the qualities they feel are important in a friend and the qualities they feel they have to offer in a friendship.

> ▸ For students to become aware of the importance of using friendships to develop joint problem-solving skills and strategies.

The focus here is on friendship and the nature of positive relationships. Students will be given the opportunity to identify the qualities of a good friend alongside assessing their own skills and attributes in this area. They will also be asked to act as an agony aunt in terms of addressing typical problems the girls may experience in relationships with friends, boyfriends and parents/carers. A central theme here is that of using friends to develop joint problem-solving skills and strategies.

Activity 1 – Thought Storming Activity

In this activity students are asked to focus on the questions: What is a friend? What does she do? What doesn't she do?

Students can either make use of the framework provided or, alternatively, the facilitator can record students' ideas on the whiteboard or flip-chart. Their contributions may include the following:

> ▸ A friend is someone who reassures me that I'm OK.

> ▸ A friend is someone who is not afraid to be different.

> ▸ A friend is someone who listens to me.

> ▸ A friend is someone who I can trust.

> ▸ A friend is always on my side.

> ▸ A friend doesn't talk behind my back.

> ▸ A friend forgives me if I make mistakes.

> ▸ A friend makes me laugh.

> ▸ A friend shows me warmth.

> ▸ A friend is someone that I can tell anything to.

Talk Time: Problem-solving Activity

Students are presented with a friendship scenario in which Christina and Ashley are described as having been best friends since nursery. They are now in secondary school and have become interested in members of the opposite sex. David, who is a member of the sixth form, asks both girls to the same party on the Saturday night. He asks Christina to go to the party with him and then asks Ashley to meet him there. When Ashley arrives, to her surprise when she opens the door, David is standing there with Christina on his arm. The students are asked to consider a range of questions in order to ultimately work out how this difficult situation can be resolved to the satisfaction of both girls.

Role-play

The students are asked to work in pairs, taking on the roles of Christina and Ashley alternatively. The idea here is to work out the conversation that the two girls might have subsequent to this situation. How would they speak to each other? What would they say? How would they resolve this difficulty? Students can feedback their experiences of engaging in the role-play activity to the group as a whole once they have worked on their two scenes.

Activity 2 – Friendship Quiz

Students are then asked to interview each other, again in their pairs, in order to identify their current levels of skills. They are asked to identify how they might become a better friend in the future, i.e. what kinds of skills would they need to further develop?

Activity 3 – Agony Aunts: Focus on Relationships

In this activity students are asked to consider a range of problem letters, all of which illustrate typical scenarios that the girls themselves may have experienced in their everyday life. These include the pressure to have sex with a boyfriend, a best friend going off with your boyfriend, bullying by older girls or parents running you down. Students are asked to share ideas in the group and to formulate reply letters to each of the problem letters on the reply letters sheet provided.

Plenary

The facilitator can ask the students to focus on the following questions:

▸ How did we feel at the start of this session?

▸ How do we feel at the end of this session?

▸ What do we think we have learnt about friendships and relationships?

▸ How do we think what we have learnt may affect our relationships and friendships in the future?

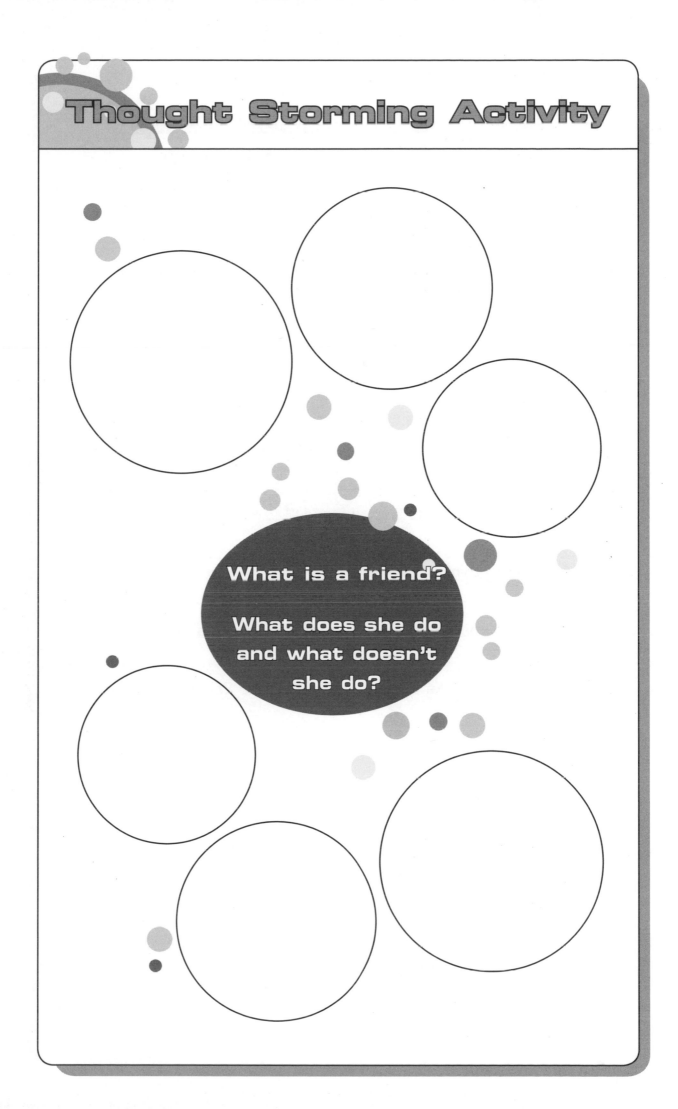

Scenario: Friendship and Relationships

Christina and Ashley have been best friends since nursery. They are now in secondary school and they have become interested in boys.

David is a sixth-former and all the girls are interested in him. There is a house party on Saturday night and David asks Christina to go to the party with him and then asks Ashley to meet him there. To Ashley's surprise, when she turns up at the party David is standing there with Christina on his arm.

Questions

- Are Ashley and Christina good friends?

- What do you think of David?

- What would you do if you were Ashley or Christina?

- Could a situation like this wreck a friendship? Should it?

- Who is to blame?

- What is more important: the friendship or David?

Friendship Quiz

Use the following questions and interview a friend. How are your skills? Are you a good friend?

1. When are you a good friend? How do you feel and what do you think, do and say?

2. What do you think a 'best friend' always does?

3. What do you think a 'best friend' never does?

4. What three things would you like your friends to know about you?

5. What three qualities would you look for in a friend?

6. What three things make you a good friend?

7. What skills do you think you could develop to be a better friend?

Pair up

Take it in turns to ask each other these questions then compare your answers. What is different and what is similar?

Do you agree?

If so, why?

If not, why?

Focus on Relationships

Dear Agony Aunt,

I am being bullied by three older girls who keep taking my money and calling me a fat cow. I am scared and depressed. What should I do?

Shakira

Dear Shakira,

Dear Agony Aunt,

My best friend has gone behind my back and is sleeping with my boyfriend. He told me but she doesn't know. What do you think I should do?

Gemma

Dear Gemma,

Dear Agony Aunt,

My boyfriend keeps on pressuring me to have sex with him. I don't mind fooling around but I don't want to have sex with him. Can you help?

Karen

Dear Karen,

Agony Aunts

Focus on Relationships, continued

Dear Agony Aunt,

My two best friends sleep around and everyone calls them slags. I feel angry because they are both really nice and I think it's up to them to do what they want to do. What should I do?

Shazia

Dear Shazia,

Dear Agony Aunt,

My mum and I used to be really close and we used to do loads of stuff together but she has no time for me now. She's got a new boyfriend and he's so annoying! I hate him! Can you help?

Sara

Dear Sara,

Dear Agony Aunt,

My little brother is blackmailing me because he saw me smoking. My dad would kill me if he found out so I have been paying my little brother off. Now, I am fed up because I never have enough money to go out. What do you advise?

Corina

Dear Corina,

Don't forget. Listen to each other and share ideas. The best solutions often result from group problem-solving.

Introduction

The facilitator can outline the main aims of this session as follows:

- For students to reflect on their own sexual activity and how this is making them feel.

- For students to become aware that there are positive and negative aspects of having sexual experiences.

- For students to outline the ways in which they can keep themselves safe or safer.

The facilitator can outline the main activities to be covered within this session, which include the thought storming activity, focusing on the positive and negative outcomes and nature of sexual activity and the notion of keeping safe.

Activity 1 – Icebreaker: Thought Storming Activity

Students are asked to focus on the following question:

What do we know about sex?

The idea here is not just to elicit technical knowledge and information but to also consider some of the statistics that may be currently available to them, for example, the growing rate of STIs and chlamydia in girls, the link between cervical cancers and early sexual activity, the link between low levels of self-esteem and promiscuity. It is important for the facilitator not to lead or impose her views in this session. The idea here is to prompt the students' thinking and to encourage them to reflect upon the nature of their own sexual activity and how this may be making them feel.

Talk Time: Problem-solving Activity

Students are presented with the scenario in which a fourteen-year old girl called Candice is becoming very curious about sex. She is currently seeing a boy called Luke who is seventeen years old and has a reputation for having sex with all the good-looking girls in the school. In this scenario Luke's family are away for the weekend and he invites Candice over to his flat. They are beginning to have sex on the sofa when the doorbell rings. Luke lets in four of his friends who have got a lot of beer and they begin to drink this and become quite drunk. Luke begins to make overtures to Candice in front of his friends, eventually whispering to her, 'Don't worry about the others – they've seen it all before.'

The students are asked to consider a range of questions and particularly focus on the way in which Candice might deal with this particular situation.

Role-play Activity

The students are divided into pairs and asked to take on the roles of Candice and Luke in order to act out the conversation that may result from this particular situation. Students are encouraged to develop a script for Candice, which will enable her to deal effectively with Luke's proposition. Students can swap roles so that both of them can have the opportunity to take on the role of each of the characters concerned. Students can finally feedback to the rest of the group how they felt about this particular activity, alongside identifying some of the suggestions that they have made in order to help Candice cope in this context.

Activity 2 – Positives and Negatives

Students are asked to work in smaller groups in order to identify the positive and negative aspects of having sex. Ideas can then be fed back to the group as a whole and the facilitator can highlight any differences and similarities in students' contributions and views.

Activity 3 – Keeping Safe

Students are presented with a range of situation cards, which can be cut out and then placed in order of safety, putting the safest situation first and the least safe situation last. This activity will require students to engage in a great deal of discussion and adequate time will need to be allocated for this. Students can then feedback to the group as a whole and the facilitator can highlight any similarities or differences in students' responses. What is most important is that students are able to consider the ways in which they can subsequently keep themselves safe or safer.

Plenary

The facilitator can ask the students to focus on the following questions:

- ▶ How did we feel at the start of this session?
- ▶ How do we feel now?
- ▶ What have we learnt about sex and keeping safe?
- ▶ How would this impact on our behaviour in the future?

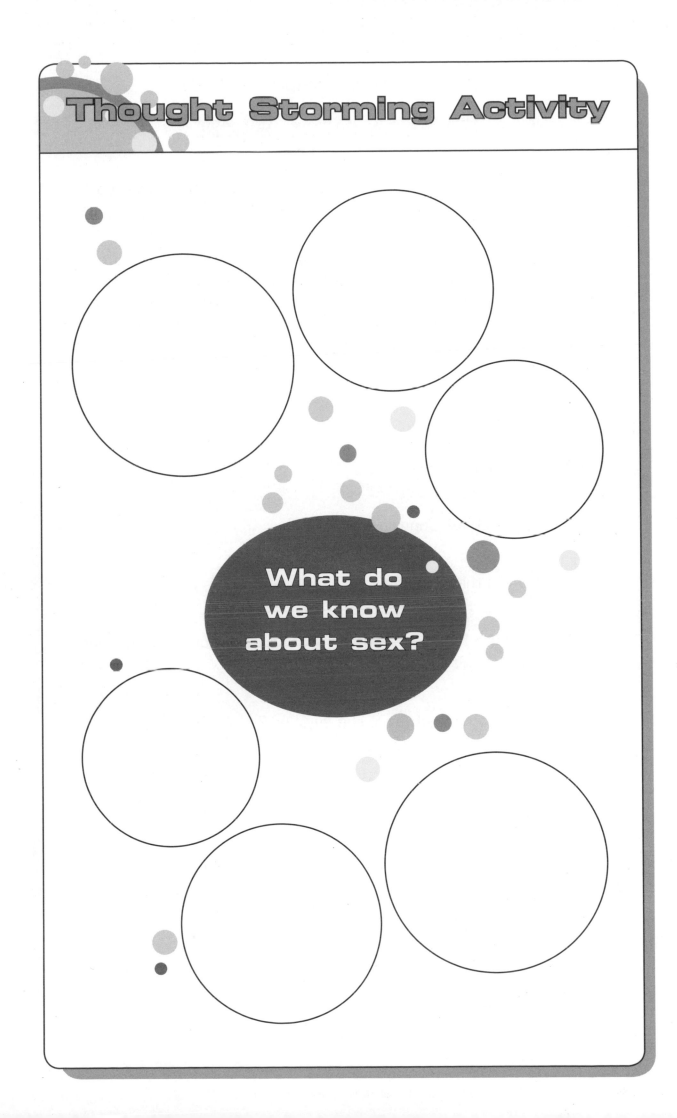

Scenario: Sex

Candice is 14 years old and very curious about sex. Candice started seeing Luke who is 17 years old and he has a reputation for having sex with the good-looking girls.

Luke's family are away for the weekend and Luke invites Candice over. They are making out on the sofa, when the doorbell rings. Luke lets in four mates, who have brought a lot of beer. As the night goes on they all drink a lot of alcohol and Luke starts to get frisky with Candice again in front of his mates. Luke whispers to Candice, "Don't worry about the others, they have seen it all before."

Questions

● What do you think Candice feels?

● What do you think of Luke?

● What will Luke and his friends think of her if she chooses to sleep with him while his friends are watching?

● What will they think of her if she says 'no'?

● What risks is she placing herself under?

● Where does this leave their relationship?

● What would you do if someone was pressurising you to do something sexually that you didn't want to do?

● If you could give Candice advice, what would it be?

Positives and Negatives

Discuss in your groups the **positives** and **negatives** of having sex.

Positives	Negatives
○ _____	○ _____
○ _____	○ _____
○ _____	○ _____
○ _____	○ _____
○ _____	○ _____
○ _____	○ _____
○ _____	○ _____
○ _____	○ _____
○ _____	○ _____
○ _____	○ _____

Keeping Safe

Cut out the **Situation Cards** and then place then in order of safety, putting the safest situation first and the least safe situation last.

Chatting on the Internet with a 36 year old man.	Getting drunk at a party and sleeping with four boys.
Having unprotected sex with your boyfriend.	Having protected sex with your partner.
Putting your photo on a chat room site.	Going to a party with older boys and taking crack.
Walking home from a party at 2:00 am.	Flirting with a younger boy that you are not really interested in.
Drinking and smoking when you are pregnant.	Forgetting to take your pill and then having sex.
Having sex with loads of boys because you know you are pregnant and it can't happen again.	Feeling angry when your mum's boyfriend touches your breast.
Going to a nightclub and letting older men buy you drinks all night.	Letting others watch you have sex.
Having sex for money.	Getting drunk and doing a strip tease at a party.

Introduction

The facilitator can outline the main aims of this session as follows:

- ▸ For students to consider the concept of a role model.

- ▸ For students to reflect on why certain people become role models and what it is about them that others admire or otherwise.

- ▸ For students to examine the difference between positive and negative role models.

It will also be important to highlight how the media plays a significant part in promoting certain individuals as role models and how they do this, for example, through advertising.

Activity 1 – Icebreaker: Thought Storming Activity

Students are asked to consider the following question:

What is a role model?

They can either make use of the activity sheet provided or, alternatively, the facilitator can record students' responses on the whiteboard or flip-chart. Contributions may include some of the following:

- ▸ someone you look up to

- ▸ someone you want to be like

- ▸ someone who is really good at what they do

- ▸ someone you admire or love

- ▸ someone who is a real success and a good person.

Talk Time: Problem-solving Activity

Students are presented with a scenario in which a girl called Vicky has apparently been compared to Victoria Beckham because she looks like her. But, unlike Victoria Beckham, Vicky is not a skinny girl and her friends have begun to call her Chunky Spice. Her friend Nimisha spends time at her house and has frequently heard her vomiting in the toilet. When she questions Vicky about this, Vicky denies it.

The students are asked to consider a range of questions in order to identify not only how both girls would be feeling but also to consider how Vicky has been pressured by the comparisons made between her and her role model and also how this situation may be resolved for her in the future.

Role-play

The students are divided into pairs and asked to take on the roles of Nimisha and Vicky in order to work out the conversation that might occur between them as a result of Vicky's behaviour. Students are asked to consider what Nimisha might say to Vicky in order to help her both admit to her problem and begin to find some kind of solution or support in order to get over it. Students are asked to take on the roles of both girls alternatively and then to feedback how they experience this activity to the rest of the group.

Activity 2 – My Heroine

The students are asked to consider who they look up to and who they would really like to be like. They are also asked to consider why they would like to be like this person. The activity sheet requires students to complete a portrait of this heroine and to record the qualities and reasons for wanting to be like them around the outside of the frame. Students may wish to share their work within the group once this has been completed.

Activity 3 – Sort and Say

Students are presented with a range of name cards, for example, Jordan, Julia Roberts, Posh Spice, Britney Spears. They are asked to discuss in the group why each of these individuals may or may not be a good or positive role model. They are asked to rank order each of the personalities, putting the best role model first and the least positive role model last. They are also asked to justify this ranking process and feed back to the group as a whole.

Plenary

The facilitator can ask the students to address the following questions:

- ▸ How did we feel at the start of this session?
- ▸ How do we feel now?
- ▸ What have we learnt about role models?
- ▸ Has what we have learnt changed our views?
- ▸ How will what we have learnt impact upon the way we perceive our role models in the future?

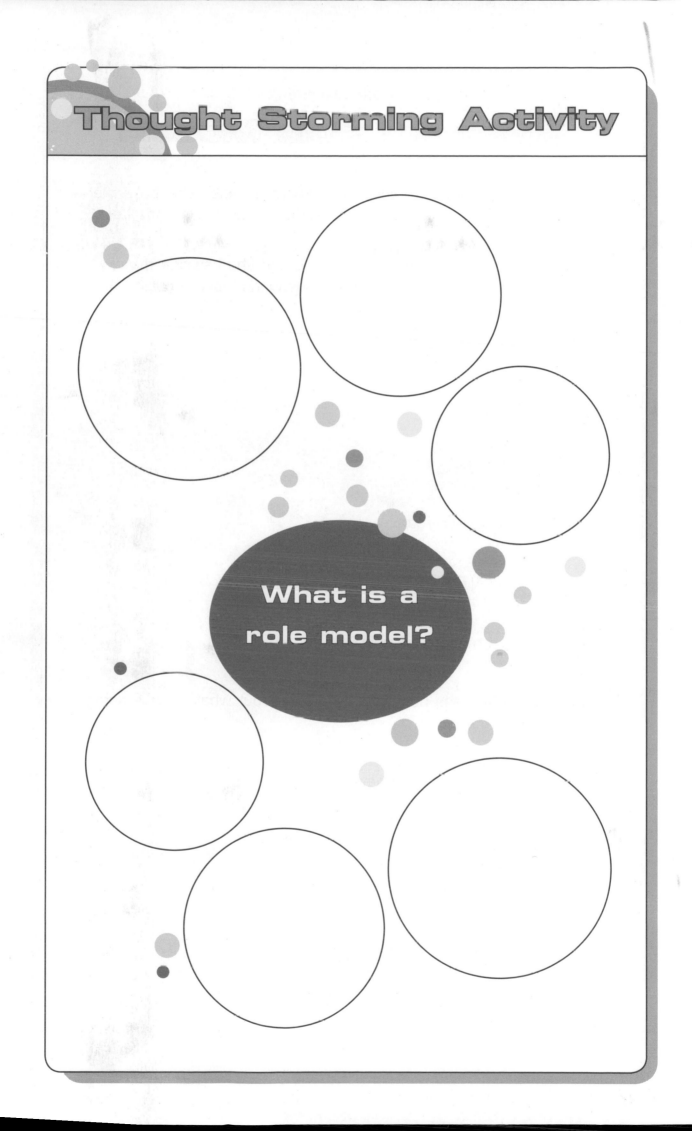

What is a
role model?

Scenario: Role Models

Vicky has been compared to Victoria Beckham because she looks like her. However, Vicky is not skinny like Victoria. In fact her friends have begun to call her Chunky Spice.

Nimisha often spends time at Vicky's house and she has heard Vicky vomiting on a few occasions. When she questions Vicky about it, she denies it.

Questions

- What is Vicky doing?

- Why is Vicky doing this?

- What should Nimisha do?

- Where could they go for help?

- If you were Nimisha how would you feel about what Vicky is doing to herself?

- What role models do you have?

- What influences do they have over your life?

My Heroine

Who do you look up to? Who would you like to be and why?

Complete the portrait and then record the person's qualities and your reasons for wanting to be like them in the boxes around the frame.

Sort and Say

Cut out the name cards below and discuss in your group why these people may or may not be positive role models. Organise the cards, putting the best role model first and the least significant role model last. Can you all agree? Why or why not?

Jordan	**Julia Roberts**
Britney Spears	**Posh Spice**
Beyonce	**Parminder Nagra**
Moira Stuart	**Margaret Thatcher**
Halle Berry	**Emma Thompson**
Cherie Blair	**Zadie Smith**
Keira Knightly	**Paula Radcliffe**

Introduction

The facilitator can outline the main aims of this session as follows:

▸ For students to become aware of key parenting skills which they may or may not have observed in their own parents/carers.

▸ For students to consider what skills they might like to use if they become parents or carers in the future.

▸ For students to understand the importance of using joint problem-solving skills, honour and empathy when experiencing difficult situations with their parents or carers.

Students are given the opportunity to problem-solve a range of difficult situations which some girls may be experiencing with their parents or carers, and the focus is again on prompting and promoting joint problem-solving skills, honour and empathy.

Activity 1 – Icebreaker: Thought Storming Activity

The students are asked to focus on the question:

What is the role of a parent?

They should contribute as many ideas as they possibly can. Responses can be recorded on the thought storming activity sheet, which can be enlarged to A3 size. Alternatively, the facilitator may wish to record students' views on the whiteboard or flip-chart. It will be interesting to highlight differences in students' perceptions and to particularly focus upon any cultural differences that may be significant. Students' contributions may include some of the following:

▸ to provide financially

▸ to provide love

▸ to give boundaries

▸ to act as a role model

▸ to teach social skills

▸ to provide physical and material goods

▸ to look after you

▸ to listen to you

▸ to stick up for you.

Talk Time: Problem-solving Activity

Students are presented with a scenario in which two parents are finding it difficult to control their seven-year old son. The main problem is that he uses inappropriate language. When his dad hears him swearing at his mum he hits him. The students are asked to consider a range of questions and to particularly focus upon whether or not physical punishment is appropriate.

Role-play

The students are divided into pairs and are asked to take on the roles of the parent, working out the conversation that might occur between them as a result of their son's behaviour. It will be important to ensure that the mum's concerns about physical violence are expressed assertively.

Activity 2 – Parenting Skills

This activity sheet requires students to consider the skills that a parent would need in order to do the job well. They are provided with a range of statements and are asked to colour code these, using:

- ▸ green for skills that they deem to be essential skills and requirements
- ▸ blue for those which they deem to be quite important
- ▸ yellow for those which they deem to be not quite so important.

It will be interesting, subsequent to this activity, to ask students to feedback and to compare and contrast their views. The facilitator should highlight those skills that all students deem to be very important, and also to highlight any significant differences in students' views.

Activity 3 – Problem Parents

In this activity students are asked to read through a range of situation cards. They are asked to consider eight girls' problems and to then place these in rank order: the worst situation first and the least worst situation last. They may then wish to go on, time allowing, to consider the kind of advice that they would give to each of the individual girls concerned and to discuss this further within the group.

Activity 4 – My Ideal Parent: The one I would like to be

In this activity students are required to illustrate themselves, i.e. how I would look as a parent, and then to write down how they would look and feel once they had taken on this role.

Once this has been completed students can compare their list with a partner, identifying any similarities or differences. They may also wish to discuss further what they think they might need to do in order to become an ideal parent in the future. It may further be helpful to consider the question:

Is there such a thing as an ideal parent?

Plenary

The facilitator can ask the students the following questions:

- ▸ How did you feel at the start of the session?
- ▸ How do you feel now the session has been completed?
- ▸ What do you think you have learnt in this session?
- ▸ How useful has this session been to you?
- ▸ What difference do you think this session will make in terms of how you act as a parent in the future?

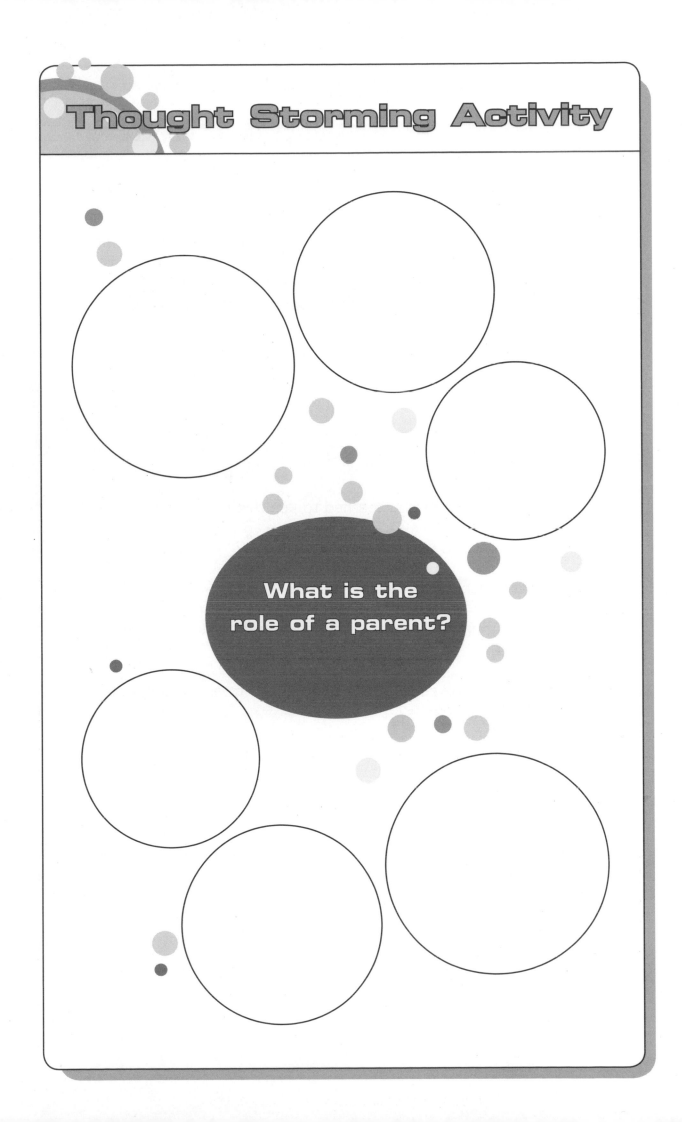

Talk Time

Scenario: Being a Parent

Nicole and Paul have a seven-year old son named Peter. Peter doesn't listen when his parents tell him not to swear.

The other day Peter was playing with the neighbour's children and he didn't get his way when he wanted to stay out later. Nicole had called him in four times to come for dinner when Peter screamed, 'Piss off!' Paul heard his inappropriate language towards Nicole and proceeded to smack him.

Paul is always using physical violence to reprimand Peter. Nicole is unsure how she feels about this.

Questions

- Where do you think Peter learned to use this language?

- Is it appropriate to use this sort of language?

- If you were Nicole, what would you do?

- When is it appropriate to use physical punishment, or is it ever appropriate?

- What other things could Nicole and Paul do to encourage Peter to follow their instructions?

- Why do you think Paul chooses to use physical punishment?

- Nicole is unsure about using physical punishment with Peter, how can she raise her concerns with Paul without offending him?

- Do you think it's important that Nicole and Paul have an agreement on how they will parent Peter?

- How do you think you would choose to discipline your child?

- What do you think makes a good parent?

- What sorts of support do you think parents need? Friends? School? Family? Outside agencies?

Parenting Skills

What skills do you think a parent/carer needs in order to do the job well?

Colour code the following statements using:

GREEN   = essential/necessary skills

BLUE   = quite important skills

YELLOW   = skills that are not quite as important

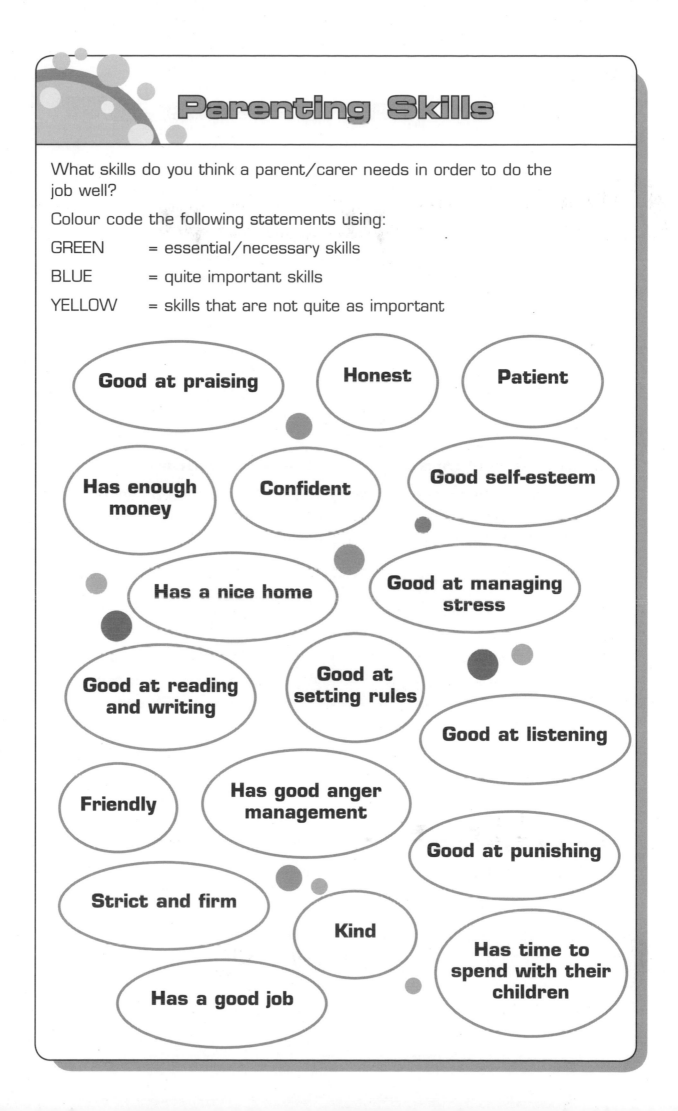

Good at praising

Honest

Patient

Has enough money

Confident

Good self-esteem

Has a nice home

Good at managing stress

Good at reading and writing

Good at setting rules

Good at listening

Friendly

Has good anger management

Good at punishing

Strict and firm

Kind

Has time to spend with their children

Has a good job

Problem Parents

Look at the situation cards below. Discuss these in your groups and place them in rank order: worst situation first and least worst situation last.

Bella's parents... Keep on telling her that she is ugly and fat and will never get a boyfriend.	**Sophie's parents...** Have 12 children and her mum is pregnant again. They have three bedrooms and it will be three years before they get another house.
Charlie's parents... Take drugs all the time and there is no money left for basics such as clothes and food.	**Claire's parents...** Argue all the time and her dad always hits her mum. He broke her nose last week.
Fozia's parents... Treat her like a second-class citizen and make her do all the housework so she doesn't have any time to see her friends or do school work.	**Gita's parents...** Won't let her go out with her friends or have a boyfriend until she is 21 as they are very strict and religious.
Kirsty's parents... Are always in the pub and leave her to take care of her siblings including six month old michael. Kirsty is 12 years old.	**Charlene's parents...** Make her do four hours extra homework every night including weekends as they want her to go to university.

My Ideal Parent

The one I would like to be

Stop, Think and Reflect

Draw	**Write**
How would I look...	What I would feel...
	○ _____
	○ _____
	○ _____
	○ _____
	○ _____
	○ _____
	○ _____
	○ _____
	○ _____

Compare your list with a partner. What is similar and different? What do you think you will need to do in the future to become an **ideal parent**?

Session 9

Drugs and Alcohol

Introduction

The facilitator can outline the main aims of this session as follows:

> ▸ For students to reflect on current knowledge about drugs and alcohol.

> ▸ For students to consider the dangers and so-called delights of drugs and alcohol.

> ▸ For students to identify ways in which girls can avoid the kind of drug and alcohol abuse which might lead them to becoming addicted or at risk of self-harm.

Activity 1 – Icebreaker: Thought Storming Activity

Students can initially focus on the question:

What do we know about drugs and alcohol?

Students should identify all the facts that are currently available to them. This can include factual information gleaned from available literature, as well as so-called 'street information'. It may be helpful for the facilitator to have some literature available for students, which specifically identifies current statistics of the link, for example, between mental health problems and drug abuse. Students' ideas and contributions can be recorded on the thought storming activity sheet or, alternatively, the facilitator may wish to write these up onto the whiteboard or flip-chart.

Talk Time: Problem-solving Activity

Students are presented with a scenario in which two girls named Janice and Simone go out on a Saturday night and get two older boys to buy them drinks. One of the boys, named Ricky, tries to persuade Simone to take some drugs.

The students are asked to consider a range of questions in order to try and find a solution to this problem and to also consider how safe the girls are in this situation.

Role-play

The students are divided into pairs and are asked to take on the roles of Simone and Ricky. They are asked to consider what Simone might say to Ricky when he is encouraging her to take the drugs. They are asked to try and identify what the best possible outcome would be in this situation.

Activity 2 – What Do You Think?

In this activity students are asked to record their own ideas as to the dangers and delights of both alcohol and drug abuse. They can then compare their ideas with others in the group and see if they are in agreement, identifying the reasons for any agreement and the reasons for any disagreements between them.

Activity 3 - Keep Safe

This activity asks students to design their own posters in order to inform girls about the difficulties and dangers associated with drug and alcohol abuse. They are asked to make up their own catch phrases in order to both attract and stimulate interest. A drawing frame is provided for this purpose.

Plenary

The facilitator can ask the students to focus on the following questions:

- ▶ How did we feel at the start of this session?

- ▶ How do we feel at this stage of the session?

- ▶ What do we think we have learnt about drugs and alcohol?

- ▶ How do we think that this knowledge may affect our behaviour, if at all?

- ▶ What advice would we give to younger girls in this area?

Thought Storming Activity

What do we know about drugs and alcohol?

Scenario: Drugs and Alcohol

Janice and Simone have been anxiously waiting for the weekend as there is a new club opening up and all their friends are going on Saturday night. They are planning to dress up to look older so they can get in.

As the bouncer nods them in past the front gate they give each other a quick hug and Simone says, 'We did it. Let's go get a drink!' At the bar, two hot guys offer to buy their drinks. As the night wears on they are drinking more and more and they haven't even opened their purses! Both girls are so excited that these guys are really into them. One of the guys, Ricky, says to Simone, 'I can see you are into enjoying yourself, how about taking some of this to heighten your enjoyment?' as he dangles a small packet of white powder in front of her face. Janice is totally wrecked by this point and Simone is a bit worried that her friend can't help her out with this decision.

Questions

- What do you think happens next?

- What do you think Simone should do?

- What do you think these guys will do if she says no?

- Do you think these guys are really into them?

- Is this a typical girl's night out?

- Are they safe? List the risks that they are taking.

- Do you think that she is under pressure to take these drugs?

- Is it necessary to drink or take drugs to have a good night out?

What Do You Think?

Record your ideas

Dangers of alcohol and drugs	**Delights** of alcohol and drugs
○ _____	○ _____
○ _____	○ _____
○ _____	○ _____
○ _____	○ _____
○ _____	○ _____
○ _____	○ _____
○ _____	○ _____
○ _____	○ _____
○ _____	○ _____
○ _____	○ _____

Compare your ideas.

Are you in agreement with others?

Why or why not?

Keep Safe

Design a poster to inform girls about the difficulties and dangers associated with drugs and alcohol abuse. Try to make up your own catch phrase. For example, 'Don't do Drugs', 'Avoid Alcohol Abuse'.

Use the drawing frame below.

Session 10
Evaluation and Looking Forward

Introduction

The facilitator can outline the main aims of this session as follows:

▸ For students to review and reflect on what has been learnt on the course.

▸ For students to decide on their own Bill of Rights, thereby stating how they feel they should be treated in life and how others should be treated.

▸ For students to envisage their preferred future and what they need to do to get there.

The students will complete an evaluation feedback form, and there will be an opportunity to present congratulation certificates to each of the individuals on the course in order to mark their successful participation in the Girl's World programme.

Activity 1 – Icebreaker: Thought Storming Activity

The students are asked to focus on the question:

What have we learnt in Girl's World?

Ideas and feedback can be recorded on the activity thought storming sheet provided or, alternatively, the facilitator may wish to make use of the whiteboard or flip-chart. It may be helpful to prompt contributions by outlining the main topics covered in the course. Key skills that may be included are as follows:

▸ skills of self-reflection

▸ skills of self-awareness

▸ empathy

▸ emotional literacy

▸ self-esteem

▸ positive thinking

▸ coping with peer pressures

▸ assertiveness

▸ friendship skills

▸ coping with sexuality

▸ identifying positive and negative role models

▸ clarifying positive parenting skills

▸ identifying and clarifying the nature of drug and alcohol abuse

▸ setting targets

▸ problem-solving skills

▸ co-operation skills.

Talk Time: Problem-solving Activity

Students are presented with a scenario in which a girl called Sasha is arranging her work experience at a garage. She is being teased by Vanessa and her other friends, and called a lesbian because she is interested to doing a 'boy's job'. The students are asked to consider a range of questions in order to identify how Sasha must be feeling and how she can respond in a confident and assertive way to this kind of bullying.

Role-play

The students are divided into pairs and asked to take on the roles of Sasha and Vanessa and to work out the conversation they might have as a result of Vanessa's put down. Students are asked to consider what she might say in order to stop them from continuing with this abuse.

Activity 2 – Bill of Rights

This handout contains a Bill of Rights for girls, which identifies key rights that girls should probably have access to. Students are asked to reflect upon this Bill of Rights and to discuss it in the group prior to having a go at making up their own Bill of Rights. It would be interesting to note any agreement or disagreement on the contents and to highlight these during a subsequent discussion.

Activity 3 – My Preferred Future

In this activity the students are asked to imagine themselves in ten years' time: identifying where they would like to be, how they would like to feel, what they would like to be doing and where they would like to be living and working. They are asked to record these ideas around a portrait in which they have detailed how they will look in ten years' time. They are finally asked to think of three things they could be doing now in order to fulfil their dreams of the future. Students can be provided with an opportunity to discuss their work with a partner or within the group as a whole, as appropriate.

Activity 4 – Evaluation of the Girl's World Programme

In this two-part evaluation the students are asked to rate each of the sessions on a scale of 1 – 10 (1 = not good, 5 = OK, 10 = excellent). They are then asked to rate the activities in the same way, i.e. thought storming activities, talk time/problem-solving activities, role-plays, worksheets and plenary sections of each session.

They are finally asked to identify the things that they enjoyed most and least and to advise the course facilitator as to how the course could be made better if it was run again in the future.

Plenary

This plenary session should allow the course facilitator to feed back to the students as to how they feel the course has gone and also provides an opportunity for the facilitator to highlight significant pieces of learning that they think have been very successful during the course. It is also an opportunity for the course facilitator to congratulate each of the girls for having made a contribution to the sessions and to the course as a whole. Celebration certificates can be awarded to each individual, signed by the facilitator, after having been photocopied onto good quality card.

Thought Storming Activity

What have we learnt in Girl's World?

Scenario: Confidence

Sasha is really interested in cars and is considering doing her work experience at a garage. All the other girls want to do hairdressing.

One day Sasha and her friends were hanging out at lunch, filling in their forms for work experience when Vanessa asks Sasha, 'So, I hear you want to work in a garage. What do you want to do that for? That is a boy's job!'

Then the other girls start chipping in, 'Yeah, what are you, a lesbian? No guy will want you!'

Sasha stands up and says, 'It's something I've always wanted to do and if you were my friends you would back off!'

Questions

- Do you think Sasha is confident?

- Do you think her friends are confident? Why or why not?

- What would you do in this situation?

- Can you give an example of a situation in which you stood up for what you believed in?

- How can you judge whether someone is confident or not?

- Is a confident person aggressive or assertive?

- Is being confident always a good thing?

- Do you think it's important to be confident?

Bill Of Rights

A Bill of Rights for Girls

I have the right...

- To feel safe all the time.

- To have my questions answered.

- To decide for myself what I would like to do.

- To be listened to.

- To have my feelings respected.

- To be myself.

- To be different.

- To be given the same opportunities as everyone else.

- To change my mind.

- To say 'no'.

- To choose my beliefs and values.

- To ask for help.

- To make mistakes and take risks.

- To be offered more than one chance.

- To take responsibilities for my actions.

Reflect and discuss this Bill of Rights in your group.

Then have a go at making up your own Bill of Rights.

Can you agree on the contents?

My Preferred Future

Try to imagine yourself in ten years' time. Where would you like to be? How do you want to feel? What do you want to be doing? Where would you want to live and work?

Sketch your 'Ten Years Forward' portrait and record your ideas around the picture frame.

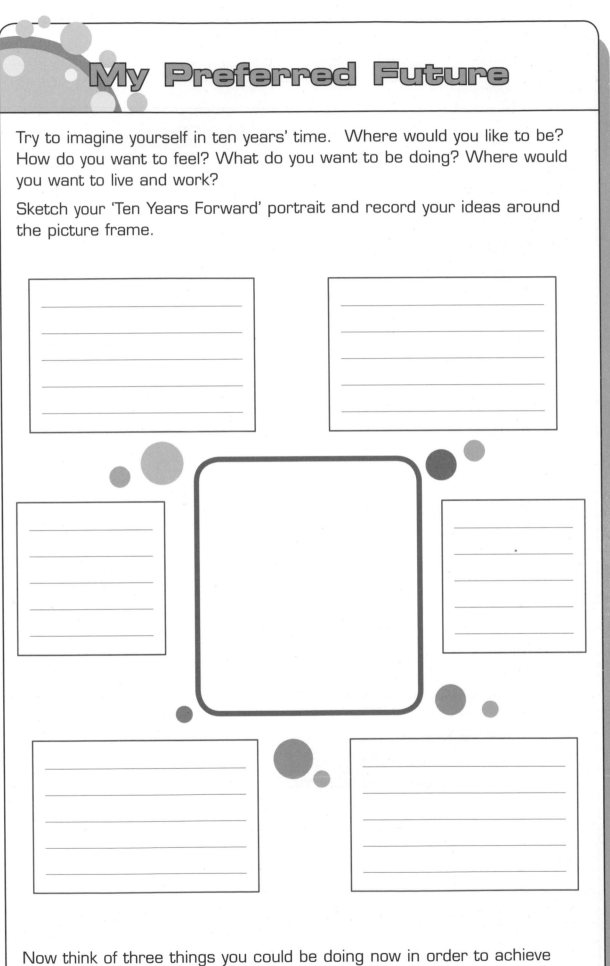

Now think of three things you could be doing now in order to achieve your future goals. Work with a partner and share your ideas.

Evaluation of Girl's World

Looking at you

Rate yourself on a scale of 1 to 10 (1=not good, 5=okay, 10=excellent) for how well you think you have developed your skills in each of the following areas. Please circle your choice.

Your level of self-esteem
1 2 3 4 5 6 7 8 9 10

Your ability to think positively
1 2 3 4 5 6 7 8 9 10

Your ability to cope with peer pressure
1 2 3 4 5 6 7 8 9 10

Your overall level of emotional literacy
1 2 3 4 5 6 7 8 9 10

Your ability to make and sustain positive relationships
1 2 3 4 5 6 7 8 9 10

Your understanding of role models
1 2 3 4 5 6 7 8 9 10

You awareness of what it is to be a good parent/carer
1 2 3 4 5 6 7 8 9 10

Your understanding of drugs and alcohol abuse
1 2 3 4 5 6 7 8 9 10

Your knowledge of safe sex
1 2 3 4 5 6 7 8 9 10

Your ability to keep motivated and set realistic targets
1 2 3 4 5 6 7 8 9 10

Evaluation of Girl's World

Looking at the course activities

Use the same scale to rate the following activities:

Thought storming activities   1 2 3 4 5 6 7 8 9 10

Talk time/problem-solve   1 2 3 4 5 6 7 8 9 10

Role-plays   1 2 3 4 5 6 7 8 9 10

Activity sheets   1 2 3 4 5 6 7 8 9 10

Plenary   1 2 3 4 5 6 7 8 9 10

What did you enjoy the most?
Why?

What did you enjoy the least?
Why?

If we ran the course again, what advice would you give us in order to make it better?

Thank you for your help and advice!

Certificate
of
Achievement

This certificate is awarded to

in recognition of valuable
contributions to Girl's World

Signature

Date

Signature

Date